Songs

Level 6 – Orange

Helpful Hints for Reading at Home

The graphemes (written letters) and phonemes (units of sound) used throughout this series are aligned with Letters and Sounds. This offers a consistent approach to learning, whether reading at home or in the classroom.

HERE IS A LIST OF PHONEMES FOR THIS PHASE OF LEARNING. AN EXAMPLE OF THE PRONUNCIATION CAN BE FOUND IN BRACKETS.

Phase 5			
ay (day)	ou (out)	ie (tie)	ea (eat)
oy (boy)	ir (girl)	ue (blue)	aw (saw)
wh (when)	ph (photo)	ew (new)	oe (toe)
au (Paul)	a_e (make)	e_e (these)	i_e (like)
o_e (home)	u_e (rule, cube)		

Phase 5 Alternative Pronunciations of Graphemes			
a (hat, what)	e (bed, she)	i (fin, find)	o (hot, so, other)
u (but, unit)	c (cat, cent)	g (got, giant)	ow (cow, blow)
ie (tied, field)	ea (eat, bread)	er (farmer, herb)	ch (chin, school, chef)
y (yes, by, very)	ou (out, shoulder, could, you)		

HERE ARE SOME WORDS WHICH YOUR CHILD MAY FIND TRICKY.

Phase 5 Tricky Words			
oh	their	people	Mr
Mrs	looked	called	asked
could			

TOP TIPS FOR HELPING YOUR CHILD TO READ:

- Allow children time to break down unfamiliar words into units of sound and then encourage children to string these sounds together to create the word.

- Encourage your child to point out any focus phonics when they are used.

- Read through the book more than once to grow confidence.

- Ask simple questions about the text to assess understanding.

- Encourage children to use illustrations as prompts.

This book focuses on /ee/ and /e_e/ and is an Orange level 6 book band.

Can you fill in the gaps?

concre_e

the_e park

dele_e

e_ening

There are lots of different songs. Songs can get people feeling sadness or glee. What songs do you like?

You might not like all songs that you hear, but you do not need to. People do not agree on what the best song is. You are free to like what you like!

Some songs are serene and slow. You can sway along to these songs. Hearing these songs at night can send you to sleep.

Serene means relaxing.

Some songs are not serene at all. An extreme song might have loud drums and screaming sounds in it.

Some songs get people tapping their feet to the beat. Songs with a fast beat are fun to bop to.

Do you tap along to the beat?

A film might have a song that plays a lot. This is a theme song. You might hear a theme song at the start or end of a film.

Singing is a talent. Some people are good singers, but they have to do it all the time to get better.

Songs often have a theme. This is what the song is about.

The different sounds and themes in a song might make people think about different things.

Songs can be long or short. They can have electronic noises or noises from keys or strings.

An artist can spend weeks, or even years, on one song. They have to think of what they want to say in the song and what sort of beat to use.

An artist may need much longer than that to complete an album.

©2023 **BookLife Publishing Ltd.**
King's Lynn, Norfolk, PE30 4LS, UK

ISBN 978-1-80505-079-7

All rights reserved. Printed in China.
A catalogue record for this book is
available from the British Library.

Songs
Written by Charis Mather
Designed by Lucy Otter

An Introduction to BookLife Readers...

Our Readers have been specifically created in line with the London Institute of Education's approach to book banding and are phonetically decodable and ordered to support each phase of the Letters and Sounds document.

Each book has been created to provide the best possible reading and learning experience. Our aim is to share our love of books with children, providing both emerging readers and prolific page-turners with beautiful books that are guaranteed to provoke interest and learning, regardless of ability.

BOOK BAND GRADED using the Institute of Education's approach to levelling.

PHONETICALLY DECODABLE supporting each phase of Letters and Sounds.

EXERCISES AND QUESTIONS to offer reinforcement and to ascertain comprehension.

CLEAR DESIGN to inspire and provoke engagement, providing the reader with clear visual representations of each non-fiction topic.

AUTHOR INSIGHT:
CHARIS MATHER

Charis Mather is a children's author at BookLife Publishing who has a love for reading and writing. Her studies in linguistics and experiences working with young readers have given her a knack for writing material that suits a range of ages and skill levels. Charis is passionate about producing books that emphasise the fun in reading and is convinced that no matter how much you already know, there is always something new to learn.

This book focuses on /ee/ and /e_e/ and is an Orange level 6 book band.

Image Credits Images are courtesy of Shutterstock.com. With thanks to Getty Images, Thinkstock Photo and iStockphoto. Cover – Ash Pollard, CosmoVector, Golden Vector, poltu Shyamal, yukipon. 2-3 – dourleak, elesi, Antlii, OlegRi. 4-5 – DmitryStock, Prostock-studio. 6-7 – Ronald Sumners, strelka. 8-9 – Anton27, fizkes. 10-11 – Africa Studio, Monkey Business Images. 12-13 – Brian Goodman, Natalja Mizinova. 14-15 – AnnaStills, CGN089.